NOBODY LIKES FROGS

A Book of Toadally Fun Facts

Barbara Davis-Pyles   Illustrated by Liz Wong

little bigfoot

an imprint of sasquatch books
seattle, wa

Wait. What?

Um . . . that isn't burping. It's croaking! Frogs
croak to find friends and scare rivals.

Did you know that frog croaks can be heard a mile away?

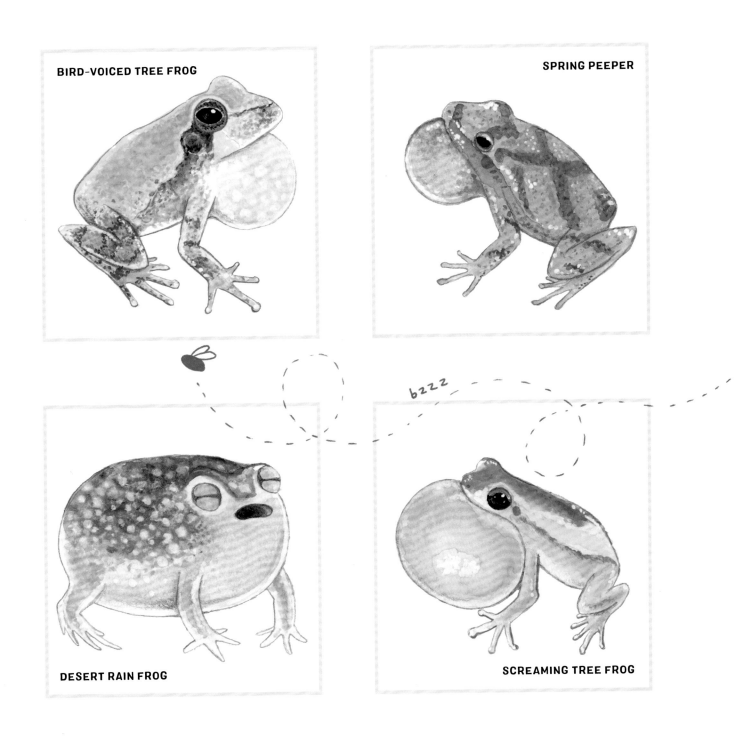

BIRD-VOICED TREE FROG

SPRING PEEPER

DESERT RAIN FROG

SCREAMING TREE FROG

bzzz

Actually, different kinds of frogs make different sounds. Not all of them sound like burps! Some sound like peeps. And some sound like whistles!

Uh . . . frogs aren't trying to do ballet.
Leaping is the way they move!

Those great leaps help frogs catch food and keep them from being food! A giant jump is the best way to get away.

What about it?

VIETNAMESE MOSSY FROG

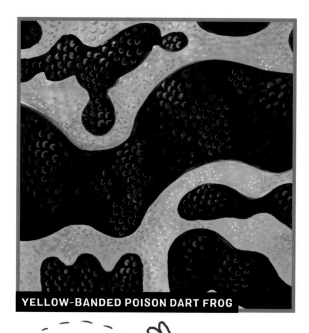

YELLOW-BANDED POISON DART FROG

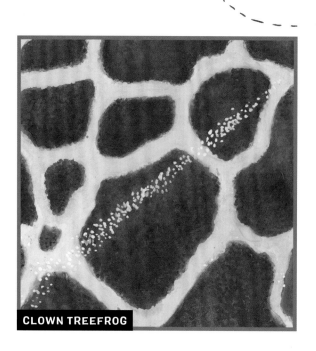

CLOWN TREEFROG

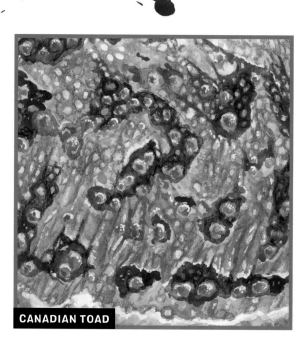

CANADIAN TOAD

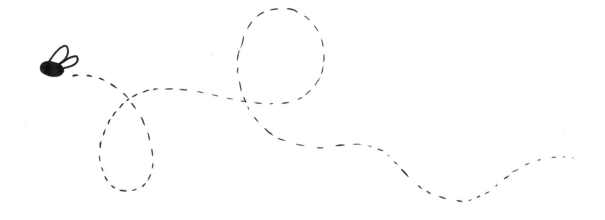

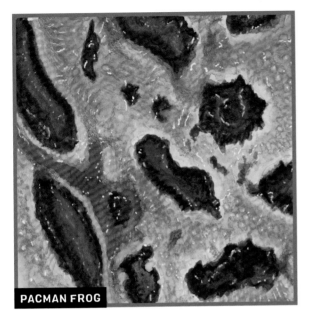

PACMAN FROG

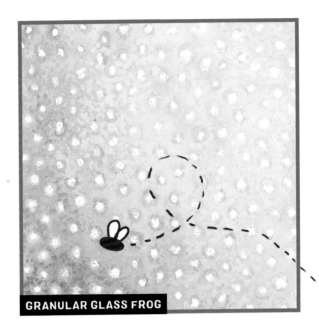

GRANULAR GLASS FROG

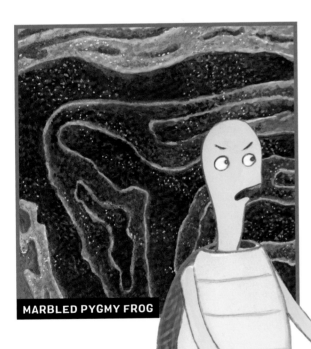

MARBLED PYGMY FROG

MALAGASY RAINBOW FROG

It's dreadful! Sometimes it's slimy. Sometimes it's warty. Without a doubt, frog hygiene is horrible!

But frog skin is supposed to be that way! Their skin protects them. It keeps their insides from drying out. In fact, frogs don't have to drink water—they get it through their skin!

They can even *breathe* through their skin when they're underwater!

But you'd be able to see all around you without even turning your head! Frog eyes are the best eyes to have! A frog's eyes even help it eat! When a frog swallows, its eyes sink in to help push the food down its throat! Isn't that *awesome?!*

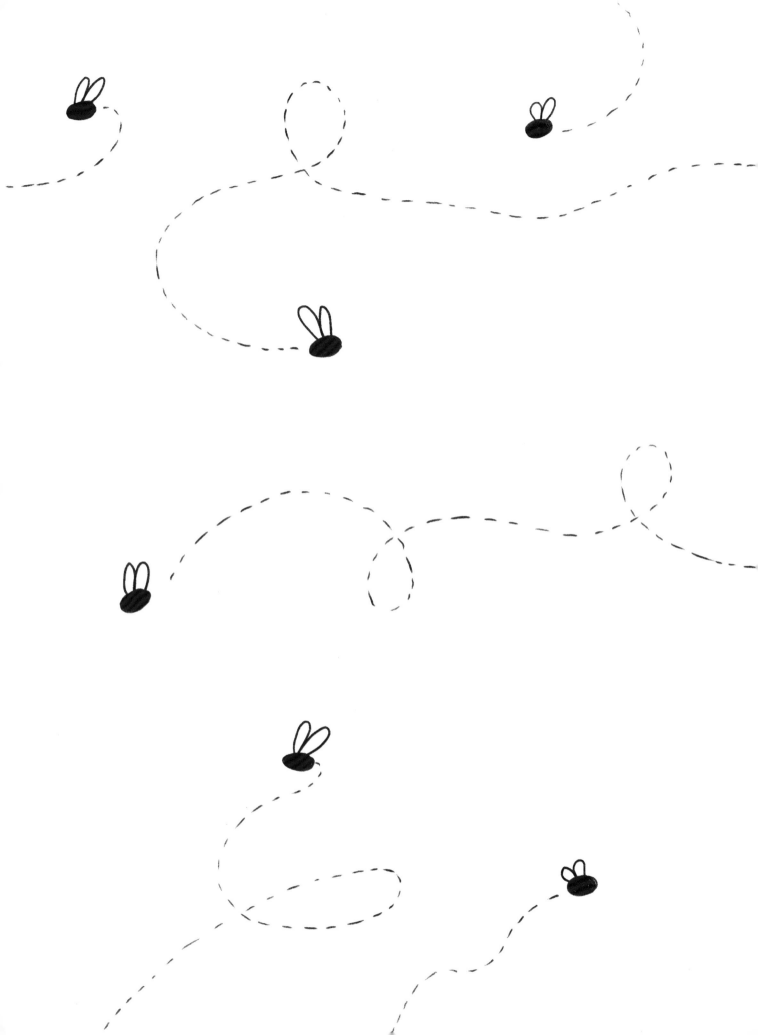

FROG FACTS

- There are over five thousand different kinds of frogs in the world!
- Sadly, about two hundred kinds of frogs have gone extinct since the 1970s.
- Frogs can be found on every continent except Antarctica.
- Frogs can live for about twenty years.
- A group of frogs is called an army.
- Some frogs are as tiny as your pinky toe.
- The goliath frog is as big as a cat!
- Every week or so, a frog sheds its skin . . . and eats it.

BE SOMEBODY WHO *LIKES* FROGS BY HELPING THEM!

- Clean up trash in storm drains and near waterways.
- Do not flush medicines or household cleaners down the toilet.
- Use less water. For example, turn off the tap while you brush your teeth.
- Ask your parents to use organic lawn-care products.
- Talk to your parents about letting some of your lawn grow naturally without mowing or raking it. Long grasses and fallen leaves stay wet longer, so they help frogs keep their skin moist. They also provide great places for frogs to find food and hide from predators.
- Finally, adding a small pond to your yard is a great family project and especially *frog*-tastic!

For Mom and Dad with love.
And for David across the pond . . .
with apologies.
–BARBARA DAVIS-PYLES

For Eric.
–LIZ WONG

Manufactured in China by C&C Offset Printing Co. Ltd.
Shenzhen, Guangdong Province, in November 2022

LITTLE BIGFOOT with colophon is a registered
trademark of Penguin Random House LLC

27 26 25 24 23   9 8 7 6 5 4 3 2 1

Editors: Ben Clanton & Christy Cox
Production editor: Peggy Gannon
Designer: Anna Goldstein

Library of Congress Cataloging-in-
Publication Data is available.

ISBN: 978-1-63217-504-5

Sasquatch Books
1325 Fourth Avenue, Suite 1025
Seattle, WA 98101

SasquatchBooks.com